WT

The Wildlife Trusts Guide to

# GARDEN
# WILDLIFE

Series Editor Nicholas Hammond

Illustrated by
Sandra Doyle, Stuart Carter
and David Daly

NEW HOLLAND

First published in 2002 by
New Holland Publishers (UK) Ltd
London • Cape Town • Sydney • Auckland

10 9 8 7 6 5 4 3 2 1

Garfield House, 86–88 Edgware Road, London
W2 2EA, United Kingdom
Website: www.newhollandpublishers.com
80 McKenzie Street, Cape Town 8001, South Africa
Level 1/Unit 4, 14 Aquatic Drive, Frenchs Forest,
NSW 2086, Australia
218 Lake Road, Northcote, Auckland, New Zealand

ISBN 1 85974 961 5

Publishing Manager: Jo Hemmings
Project Editor: Mike Unwin
Production: Joan Woodroffe
Bird Artwork: David Daly

**Packaged by Wildlife Art Ltd:**
www.wildlife-art.co.uk
Design and Cover Design: Sarah Crouch
Art/Copy Editor: Sarah Whittley
Proof-reading and Index: Rachel Lockwood
Illustrators: Sandra Doyle, Stuart Carter
and Dr Michael Roberts

Reproduction by Modern Age
Repro Co. Ltd, Hong Kong
Printed and bound in Singapore by
Kyodo Printing Co (Singapore) Pte Ltd

# Contents

Since 1912, The Wildlife Trusts have been speaking out for wildlife and undertaking practical action at the local level throughout the UK. Believing that wildlife is essential to a healthy environment for all, The Wildlife Trusts work with people from all walks of life – communities, industry, government, landowners, and families – to make sure nature gets a chance amongst all of the pressures of the modern world.

With years of experience and the service of the UK's top naturalists, The Wildlife Trusts and Wildlife Watch – the UK's leading club for young environmentalists – play a key part in restoring the balance between new developments and the natural world. With the specialist skills of volunteers and staff they manage more than 2,300 wildlife reserves (totalling more than 80,000 hectares), which are among the finest sites in the UK.

Their members, who number more than 340,000, contribute to their achievements by their generosity and hard work, and by spreading the message to everyone that wildlife matters.

The Wildlife Trusts is a registered charity (number 207238). For membership, and other details, please phone The Wildlife Trusts on 0870 0367711 or log on to www.wildlifetrusts.org

Gardens in northern Europe are wonderful places to start watching wildlife. This book is intended for the person who wants to try to identify the animals that appear in the garden. This book cannot be comprehensive since there are so many species that might turn up in gardens. The animals that are seen in gardens will vary from season to season. It is well-known that some birds migrate southwards in winter and return to breed in spring. Several species move into gardens in search of food in winter and then disappear in spring when they return to woodlands and other habitats to breed. Other animals also disappear from view in some seasons. This does not necessarily mean that they have left the garden: they may be hibernating or continuing their lives away from our view.

Animals have over millions of years adapted to make the most of their particular environment. In the case of some species of invertebrates the habitat to which they have adapted is small and specialised, often confining themselves to a certain food plant.

Gardens are somewhat artificial, but they will have obvious traces of the habitats which they have replaced. Where houses have been built in what was once woodland, the gardens sometimes contain mature oak trees, which attract species of birds and insects not found in other gardens. Where houses have been built on farmland there may be the remnants of hedges, with their characteristic woodland edge fauna.

## Food and behaviour

Food, shelter and reproduction are the keys to an animal's survival. The requirement for food is obvious and, since this is also the area where gardeners and wildlife are most likely to find themselves at odds, these are important factors in identifying the species. Some of the animals that come into gardens can be pests, because they eat the plants grown by gardeners. Others, on the other hand, could be encouraged because they feed on the pest species and provide at least some control over their numbers. Animals occur at different seasons. An obvious example is the swallow, which appears in March or April and disappears in September or October, because

it is a migrant. The swallow breeds in Europe and when the insects it eats become scarce, it flies south for the winter. Other birds may change their feeding habits to cope with the changes of food from season to season. Blackbirds, for example, concentrate on earthworms, insects and other invertebrates when they are plentiful in the summer, but will turn to berries and fruit in autumn and winter. It is in winter when food is scarce that birds will be attracted to gardens. Great tits and blue tits descend on gardens in winter in large numbers, making the rounds of garden bird feeders. In spring, most move away from gardens to their breeding grounds in woodlands, where there are many insects that will provide food when their young hatch.

The peacock is a common garden butterfly, especially if there are nettles on which the caterpillars might feed. The first peacocks are seen as the weather warms in March and they emerge from hibernation to breed. After May they seem to disappear, because the adults have bred and the new generation is going from eggs to larvae to pupae to finally emerge as butterflies from July to September. On sunny autumn days they will be seen feeding on the nectar of the last michaelmas daisies or juices of rotting windfall fruit, before hibernating throughout the winter. In the depths of winter you might come across one in a corner of the garden shed or even in the house. The life cycle of all insects includes a number of stages, which take an insect throughout the year from egg to the adult insect. These stages vary between species in terms of the timing, but each cycle is timed to provide the maximum opportunity for the larvae to feed.

Reproduction is, of course, a vital part of the lives of animals. Birds sing in the spring to proclaim that they hold a territory and to attract a mate. The flight of male brimstone butterflies on warm spring mornings has the same purpose. You will notice other butterflies and dragonflies patrolling your garden in search of a mate. Having paired, birds find places in which to build nests and rear young, which means that there has to be sufficient food for their offspring. Insects have to find the food plants on which their larvae can feed or, if they are predatory, enough of their prey.

## Making a garden fit for wildlife

A pristine garden, in which pesticides and herbicides are used extensively and where lawns are cut to provide a neat sward like a billiard table, is not likely to attract much wildlife. That doesn't mean that your garden has to be a wilderness. Indeed, if a garden is left to run riot, it may eventually become attractive to a smaller variety of wildlife than a well-managed garden, in which consideration is given to wildlife.

If you garden in a non-harmful, "organic" way, avoiding using herbicides or pesticides, you will attract wildlife, even though you have a conventional, short-cut lawn and formal herbaceous borders. During the breeding season, try to minimise disturbance to hedges where birds nest, and to compost heaps, which provide refuge to a host of wildlife from hedgehogs and grass snakes to earthworms and centipedes. Discourage cats, which are the greatest killers of garden wildlife.

To attract any wildlife a garden must have food and shelter. It is possible to attract birds to the smallest garden by putting out food, such as kitchen scraps and seeds. Insects, particularly bees, hoverflies and butterflies, can be attracted by planting bushes and flowering plants from which they can extract nectar and pollen. Birds will be attracted by berry-bearing shrubs.

Shelter in the form of nestboxes will attract birds, but they will only nest if there is sufficient food available and this means small insects, because even the seed-eating birds feed their young with insects. Many insects and other invertebrates require shelter when they are not active, if you look under leaf litter, logs and stones there will be a large number. Hollow sticks held into a frame with chicken wire can provide holes in which solitary bees and wasps can nest.

Compost heaps, as well as being a positive way of re-using waste, are also an important place in which invertebrates will live and breed. A compost heap may also provide hibernation places for hedgehogs, grass snakes and toads.

An important feature in a wildlife garden is a pond, both to attract frogs, toads, newts and aquatic insects and to provide birds and mammals with somewhere to drink and bathe.

## Earthworm
*Lumbricus terrestris*
SIZE AND DESCRIPTION  Up to 30 cm long.
Largest worm in Europe.
HABITAT  Very common throughout Europe, Asia and
North America. Spends most of its life underground. Tunnels
can be as deep as 1.8 m.
FOOD/HABITS  Eats vegetation and animal particles found in soil. Liked by
gardeners as they increase the humus content in soil. It swallows earth,
extracting the goodness as it passes through its body. The remains are
deposited above ground as casts. Worms are hermaphrodites but they
still have a mate. This takes place on damp summer nights, where sperm
is swapped.

## Garden snail
*Helix aspersa*
SIZE AND DESCRIPTION  Large, round shell has a diameter of 25–40 mm
and a wide, round, white-lipped mouth. Brown or yellowish shell has
pale flecking and up to five darker spirals.
HABITAT  Parks, woods and wasteland in Europe. Frequently found in
gardens, where it needs shelter from the winter cold.
FOOD/HABITS  Feeds on low-growing plants. It is active at night, and
congregates during the day at regular resting places.

## White-lipped snail
*Cepaea hortensis*
SIZE AND DESCRIPTION  Shell is
14 x 17 mm, with a lip that is
usually white, sometimes
brown. Smaller than the
brown-lipped snail. Shell has up to five
dark spirals, but may have none.
HABITAT  Woods, hedges and gardens. Found throughout Europe.
FOOD/HABITS  Feeds on grass and low-growing plants, at night and after rain.

## Garden slug
*Arion hortensis*

Size and description  Up to 40 mm long. Bluish-black and
paler on the flanks, with an orange underside. Mucus is orange
or yellow.

Habitat  Most common on cultivated land, but can also be found
in woods and gardens across Europe, except the far north.

Food/Habits  Eats any plants near the ground, and is a serious
pest of strawberries, lettuces and seedlings.

## Great grey slug
*Limax maximus*

Size and description  Up to 200 mm long. Pale grey, heavily
marked with dark spots, appearing striped at the end of the
body. Short keel on rear end of the body.

Habitat  Woods, hedges and gardens.

Food/Habits  Eats fungi and rotting plant material. Mating
involves two individuals climbing a fence, tree-trunk or wall,
and then lowering themselves on a string of mucus. Each of
these hermaphrodites then lays eggs.

## Pill millipede
*Glomeris marginata*
SIZE AND DESCRIPTION  Up to 20 mm long and
3 mm wide, with 17–19 pairs of legs. Looks
like the pill woodlouse, but its dorsal plates
are shinier and deeper, and there is a broad,
almost semi-circular plate at the rear.

HABITAT  Leaf litter in woodland, hedges and gardens across Europe.
FOOD/HABITS  Eats stems and dead vegetation. Rolls up into a ball
when disturbed.

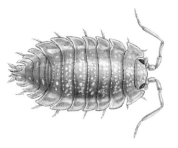

## Woodlouse
*Oniscus asellus*
SIZE AND DESCRIPTION
About 15 mm long and 8 mm wide. The body
sections are not obvious, giving the woodlouse a
smooth outline. Shiny grey in colour, with yellow
or cream blotches and pale edges to the plates
on the back.
HABITAT  Abundant across Europe.
FOOD/HABITS  Rotting wood and other plants.

## Centipede
*Lithobius forficatus*
SIZE AND DESCRIPTION
18–30 mm long and
4 mm wide. Shiny chestnut-
brown. Adults have 15 pairs
of legs; hatchlings have

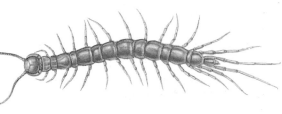

seven pairs, growing extra pairs at each moult. Head is rounded.
HABITAT  Widespread throughout Europe. Abundant in gardens.
FOOD/HABITS  Hides under stones and logs in daytime. At night,
it hunts insects, worms, and other centipedes.

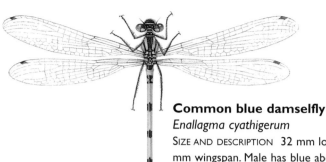

### Common blue damselfly
*Enallagma cyathigerum*
SIZE AND DESCRIPTION  32 mm long, with a 36–42 mm wingspan. Male has blue abdomen with black spots, with the 8th and 9th segments all blue. Female has a yellowish or bluish abdomen, with variable dark markings. Strong flier.
HABITAT  Near water. Found in most of Europe.
FOOD/HABITS  Flies May to September.

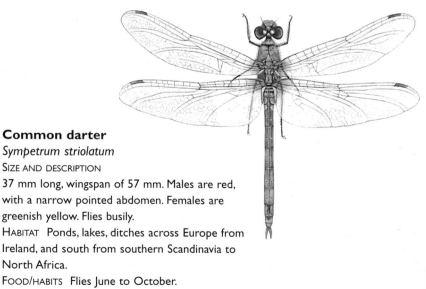

### Common darter
*Sympetrum striolatum*
SIZE AND DESCRIPTION
37 mm long, wingspan of 57 mm. Males are red, with a narrow pointed abdomen. Females are greenish yellow. Flies busily.
HABITAT  Ponds, lakes, ditches across Europe from Ireland, and south from southern Scandinavia to North Africa.
FOOD/HABITS  Flies June to October.

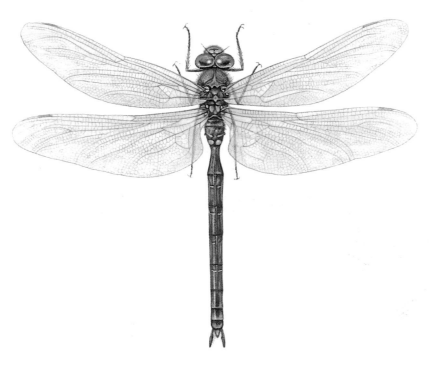

## Brown hawker
*Aeshna grandis*

SIZE AND DESCRIPTION  73 mm long, with a wingspan of 102 mm. Brown wings make this species unmistakable. Male has a brown abdomen with bright blue spots. Female has yellow markings on her brown abdomen. Both sexes have diagonal marks on the side of the thorax. Strong flier.

HABITAT  Ponds, lakes, canals, peat bogs and slow-flowing rivers. Absent from Iceland, Iberia, Italy, Greece, Scotland and northern Scandinavia.

FOOD/HABITS  Flies mid-June to mid-October. Hunts flies, mosquitoes, moths and butterflies.

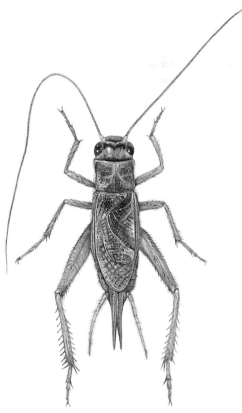

## House cricket
*Acheta domesticus*

SIZE AND DESCRIPTION Body length: 16–20 cm. Straw-coloured to brown body, with black marks on the head. Wings extend beyond the tip of the abdomen. Female has a straight ovipositor, up to 15 mm long.

HABITAT The house cricket is a native insect of Asia and Africa, but is now widespread in Europe. It lives in buildings, but may also be found at refuse tips in summer. Song is a soft warble delivered at dusk or at night.

FOOD/HABITS Feeds on refuse, but will also eat stored food.

## Common field grasshopper
*Chorthippus brunneus*

SIZE AND DESCRIPTION  Body length: 14–18 mm (m); 19–25 mm (f). Colour
can be grey, green, purple or black. Wings are narrow, and extend beyond
the tip of the abdomen. Male's abdomen has a reddish tip, a feature that
sometimes also occurs in the female. Song is a hard "sst" sound, lasting
about 0.2 seconds and repeated at 2-second intervals.

HABITAT  Widespread in dry, grassy habitats, from Scandinavia to the
Pyrenees and Italy.
Particularly common in
southern England.

FOOD/HABITS  Adults
are seen from July
to October.

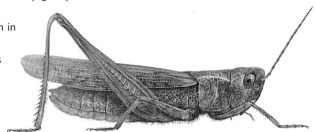

## Oak bushcricket
*Meconema thalassinum*

SIZE AND DESCRIPTION  Body length: 12–15 mm. Pale green, with wings
extending beyond the tip of the abdomen. Female has a long, upward-curving
ovipositor. Male has two thin, inward-curving cerci, about 3 mm long. Long
yellow mark down the back, with two brown flecks on either side.

HABITAT  Lives in trees, particularly oaks, but may also be found in gardens.
Distributed from southern Sweden to
northern Spain, Italy and
the Balkans.

FOOD/HABITS  Adults are
seen from July
to October.

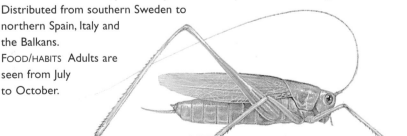

### Praying mantis
*Mantis religiosa*
SIZE AND DESCRIPTION
20 mm long. Green
body, sometimes brown.
Males are particularly slender.
HABITAT Rough grassland, scrub
and maquis in Europe, as far south
as southern France.
FOOD/HABITS Preys on other
insects. Adopts a threat display,
raising the neck and front legs in
a "praying" posture. Female
eats the male after or
during copulation.

### Green shield bug
*Palomena prasina*
SIZE AND DESCRIPTION 10–15 mm long. Bright green in
spring and summer, bronze-coloured in autumn. Wing
tips are dark brown.
HABITAT Woodland edges and glades, hedgerows and
gardens with shrubs and herbaceous borders over
much of Europe.
FOOD/HABITS Eats leaves of trees, shrubs and
herbaceous plants. Hibernates in leaf litter.

## Common earwig
*Forficula auricularia*
SIZE AND DESCRIPTION
Body length: 10–15 mm; pincers
measure 4–9 mm in the male and
4–5 mm in the female.
HABITAT Abundant throughout Europe,
in a wide range of habitats. Very
common in gardens.
FOOD/HABITS Mainly vegetarian. White
earwigs found in the garden are in the
process of moulting. Displays parental
care for its young when disturbed.

## Common flower bug
*Anthocoris nemorum*
SIZE AND DESCRIPTION 3–4 mm. Shiny
and generally brownish, with a black
spot on the greyish forewings. Head
is black.
HABITAT Found on almost any type
of tree, shrub or herbaceous plant.
Occurs over most of Europe.
FOOD/HABITS A predator of aphids, red
spider mites and other insects. Adults
hibernate under loose bark and in
clumps of grass.

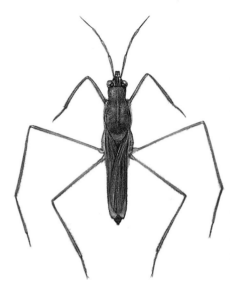

## Common pond skater
*Gerris lacustris*
SIZE AND DESCRIPTION
10 mm long. Has a broader body than the water measurer and a considerably shorter head, which has largish eyes. Usually fully-winged. Several similar species.
HABITAT Lives on the surface of slow-moving water.
FOOD/HABITS Flies away from water to hibernate. When swimming, it moves across the water's surface with a rowing action of the middle legs. The trailing hindlegs act as rudders, while the front legs catch insects that fall into the water.

## Common backswimmer
*Notonecta glauca*
SIZE AND DESCRIPTION
16 mm long. Has long, bristly hindlegs. Swims on its back, which is keeled, clutching a large air-bubble to its "underside". There are several species of water boatman.
HABITAT Swims in still water, and will fly in warm weather.
FOOD/HABITS A hunter of tadpoles, fish and insects.

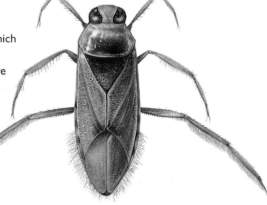

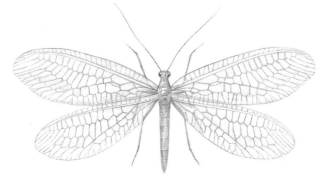

## Green lacewing
*Chrysopa pallens*

SIZE AND DESCRIPTION  15–20 mm long; wingspan of 30–40 mm. Bright green body, with bright golden eyes and green veins on transparent wings. Several species on continent; two very similar species in British Isles.

HABITAT  Woods, hedgerows, gardens and well-vegetated areas. Most of Europe.

FOOD/HABITS  Mainly nocturnal. Feeds on aphids. Flies May to August.

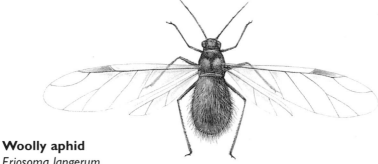

## Woolly aphid
*Eriosoma langerum*

SIZE AND DESCRIPTION  1–2 mm long. Purplish-brown, with or without wings, and covered with strands of whitish, fluffy wax.

HABITAT  Orchards and gardens across Europe. Accidentally introduced from America.

FOOD/HABITS  Sucks the sap of fruit trees. Most young are born live by parthogenesis.

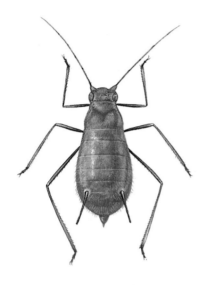

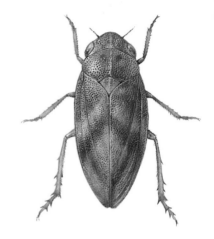

## Rose aphid
*Macrosiphum rosae*
SIZE AND DESCRIPTION  Up to 3 mm
long. Common and widespread. Colour
varies from dull-pink to green. Can
be winged and wingless.
HABITAT  Infests rose bushes in spring.
In summer migrates to other plants
such as scabious and teasels.
FOOD/HABITS  Feeds on sap from
flower bud, stem and leaves of
rose. Pest to gardeners.

## Common froghopper
*Philaenus spumarius*
SIZE AND DESCRIPTION
5 mm long. Variable brown pattern.
Wings held together like a tent. Young
coat themselves in a white broth called
"cuckoo-spit".
HABITAT  Woody and herbaceous plants
across Europe, except in the far north.
FOOD/HABITS  Flies from June to
September. Feeds on plant sap. Found
on soft herbaceous plants.

## Large white
*Pieris brassicae*

SIZE AND DESCRIPTION  Forewing is 25–35 mm. Black tips extend halfway down the forewing's edge. Upperside of forewing has two black spots in female, one in male. Underside of forewing has two spots in both sexes. Caterpillar is green, with black spots and yellow stripes.

HABITAT  Gardens and other flowery places.

FOOD/HABITS  Flies April to October. Eggs are laid on the underside of leaves. The larvae feed on brassicae and nasturtiums.

## Small white
*Pieris rapae*

SIZE AND DESCRIPTION  Forewing is 15–30 mm. Upperside is white, with one black or grey spot on male's forewing and two on female's. Black or grey forewing patches extend further along the leading edge than down the side of the wing. Two spots on underside of forewing in both sexes. Underside of hindwings is yellowish. Larva is green, with a yellow stripe along its side.

HABITAT  Gardens, hedges and flowery places across Europe. Abundant to the point of being a pest.

FOOD/HABITS  Flies March to October. Two to four broods. Eggs are laid on leaves. Larvae feed on brassicae and nasturtiums.

### Brimstone
*Gonepteryx rhamni*

SIZE AND DESCRIPTION  Forewing is 25–30 mm. Male's wings are sulphur yellow on top, but paler beneath. Female is white, with a pale green tinge, but she lacks the large white's black markings. Larva is green, with white stripes along the side.

HABITAT  Open woodland, gardens and flowery places. All Europe, but not most of Scotland and northern Scandinavia.

FOOD/HABITS  Flies February to September. Larvae eat buckthorn and alder buckthorn. Adults overwinter in holly or ivy.

## Orange tip
*Anthocaris cardamines*
SIZE AND DESCRIPTION
Forewing is 20–25 mm. Male
has orange wing-tips and
green-blotches on underside
of hindwing. Female has
greyish patches on forewing,
and mottled underwings.
HABITAT Hedgerows, gardens,
damp meadows and woodland
margins. All Europe, except south-
west or southern Spain or northern Scandinavia.
FOOD/HABITS Flies April to June. Larvae eat garlic mustard,
lady's smock, but also sweet rocket and honesty in gardens.
Overwinters as a pupa.

## Holly blue
*Celastrina argiolus*
SIZE AND DESCRIPTION Forewing of 12–18 mm.
Upperside of male is violet blue. Female is
paler blue, edged with a broad dark band. The
dark band is broader in the second brood.
Underside of the wings is pale blue-grey. The
caterpillar is small, green and slug-like. This is
the blue most likely to be seen in gardens.

HABITAT Woodland margins, hedgerows, parks and gardens. Found across
Europe, except in Scotland and northern Scandinavia.
FOOD/HABITS Flies April to September. First brood feeds on flowers and
developing fruit of holly; second (late summer) brood feeds on ivy. Adults
drink honeydew, oozing sap and juices of carrion. Winters as a pupa.

### Small copper
*Lycaena phlaeas*
SIZE AND DESCRIPTION Forewing is 10–17 mm. Bright forewing is like shiny copper, with dark flecks and brown edges. Caterpillar is small and green.
HABITAT Gardens, flowery wasteland and heathland across Europe.
FOOD/HABITS Flies February to November. Two or three broods, with adults from the third brood being rather small. Food plants for larvae are common sorrel, sheep's sorrel and docks.

### Small tortoiseshell
*Aglais urticae*
SIZE AND DESCRIPTION Forewing is 25 mm. Upperside is bright orange and black, with a row of blue spots on the trailing edge of the hindwings. Caterpillar is bristly and black.
HABITAT All kinds of flowery places. Common across the whole of Europe.
FOOD/HABITS Flies March to October. Adults overwinter, often in buildings. Larvae feed on nettles, elms and hops.

## Peacock
*Inachis io*

SIZE AND DESCRIPTION  Forewing is 30 mm. Wings have four large, peacock-like "eyes". Upperside is orange, while underside is very dark brown. Caterpillar is black and bristly, similar to small tortoiseshell only larger.

HABITAT  Flowery places, including gardens. Across Europe, and as far north as southern Scandinavia.

FOOD/HABITS  Flies March to May, and July to September. Larvae feed on nettles. Adults often overwinter in buildings.

## Red admiral
*Vanessa atalanta*
SIZE AND DESCRIPTION
Forewing is 30 mm.
Upperside is a velvety dark
brown, with bright orange
bars on each wing. Tips of
forewings are black with
white markings. Underside of
hindwing is pale brown, while
underside of forewing shows
orange, blue and white markings.
Dark caterpillar has bristles and
a pale yellow stripe along the side.
HABITAT Flowery places. Across Europe, except in far north of Scandinavia.
FOOD/HABITS Flies May to October. There are two broods. Larvae feed on
nettles. Adults feed on rotting fruit in autumn.

## Comma
*Polygonia c-album*
SIZE AND DESCRIPTION
Forewing is 23 mm. Wings
have jagged edges. Orange
upperside, with black and buff
markings. Underside of
hindwing has a white comma-
shaped mark. The black caterpillar
is sparsely bristled and has a white
rear. Looks like a bird dropping.
HABITAT Woodland margins, gardens,
hedges and other flowery places.
Common across Europe, but absent from Ireland, northern Britain and Scandinavia.
FOOD/HABITS Flies March to September. There are two broods. Larvae feed on
stinging nettles, hops and elms. Overwinters as an adult.

## Painted lady
*Cynthia cardui*
SIZE AND DESCRIPTION  Forewing is 20–25 mm.
Upperside is orange, with a black forewing tip patched
with white. Underside is pale, with three blue
underwing spots. Black caterpillar has tufts of hairs
and a yellow-and-red stripe down the side.
HABITAT  Flowery places, including roadsides and
gardens. Across Europe, but a migrant from North
Africa. Does not survive European winter.
FOOD/HABITS  Flies April to November, arriving in
Britain in late spring/early summer. Two broods in
Europe, but produces broods throughout the year
in North Africa. Eats thistles and sometimes
stinging nettles.

## Meadow brown
*Maniola jurtina*
SIZE AND DESCRIPTION
Forewing 20–26 mm.
Brown and orange with
single black eye with
a white highlight on the
upper wing. Females
larger than males. Green
larva with white stripe
along side.
HABITAT Grasslands and in
southern Europe woodlands.
Very common across Europe southwards
from southern Scandinavia.
FOOD/HABITS Flies from May to September.
Larva feeds on grasses. Winters as larva.

## Gatekeeper
*Pyronia tithonus*
SIZE AND DESCRIPTION Forewing
17–25 mm. Usually smaller than
meadow brown and with orange
patches on wings. "Eyes" are
black with two highlights. Green
or brown larva.
HABITAT Hedgerows and
woodland margins. Southern
Britain and Ireland and south across
Europe.

FOOD/HABITS Flies July to September. Larval
foodplant is fine-leaved grasses. Adult fond
of bramble blossom and marjoram.

## Wall

*Lasiommata megera*

SIZE AND DESCRIPTION  Forewing 17–25 mm. Brown and orange patterned with "eyes" on forewings. Underside of hindwing is pale silvery brown. Caterpillar is bluish-green with faint white stripes.

HABITAT  Rough grassy places and gardens. Found throughout Europe, except nothern Scotland and Scandinavia.

FOOD/HABITS  Flies March to October. Adult sunbathes on walls and fences. Foodplants are grasses. There are two to three broods. Overwinters as larva.

## Lackey moth
*Malacosoma neustria*
SIZE AND DESCRIPTION
Forewing 20 mm. Comes in a range of browns from buff to brick with two cross-lines on forewings. Similar to fox moth. Larva is long, tufted and grey-blue with white, orange, black and yellow stripes along the body.
HABITAT Orchards, gardens, woods, parks and hedges over most of Europe except Scotland and northern Scandinavia.
FOOD/HABITS Flies June to August at night. Single-brooded. Larva live in colonies in cocoons feeding on leaves of hawthorn, blackthorn, plums and sallows. Winters as egg.

## Peach blossom
*Thyatira batis*
SIZE AND DESCRIPTION Forewing about 15 mm. Forewings brown with pink blotches. Larva is dark brown with slanting white lines and bumps on back.
HABITAT Woodland and woodland edge in northern and central Europe including woodlands in British Isles.
FOOD/HABITS Flies at night May to August. Single-brooded. Larva feeds on bramble.

## Winter moth
*Operophtera brumata*
SIZE AND DESCRIPTION  Forewing about
15 mm. Greyish-brown, faintly
patterned wings in male. Female has
stunted, relict wings. Green looper
caterpillar about 20 mm long.
HABITAT  Abundant where there are
trees and shrubs.
FOOD/HABITS  Nocturnal and attracted
to lighted windows. Look for females
on windowsills and tree-trunks. Flies
October to February. Larva feeds on
fruit and other trees. Serious pest of
hard fruits causing blossom to curl.

## Magpie moth
*Abraxas grossulariata*
SIZE AND DESCRIPTION  Forewing is about
20 mm. Variable black-and-white pattern,
with a yellowish-orange line across the
middle of the forewing and near the
head. The larva, about 30 mm long, is
pale green with black spots and a rusty
line along its sides.
HABITAT  Woods, gardens and hedges
across Europe, except in the far north.
FOOD/HABITS  Flies June to August.
Larvae feed on blackthorn, currants,
hawthorn and many other shrubs.
Overwinters as a small caterpillar and
pupates in May or June.

### Privet hawk moth
*Sphinx ligustri*

SIZE AND DESCRIPTION Forewing up to 55 mm. Brown wings with black markings and tan trailing edge to forewings. Body striped with pink and black. Green caterpillar with seven purple and white stripes on each side of the body.

HABITAT Woodland edge, hedges, parks and gardens across Europe except Ireland, Scotland and far north of Scandinavia.

FOOD/HABITS Flies June to July, feeding on nectar on the wing, especially on honeysuckle. Larva feeds on privet, ash and lilac. Overwinters as pupa in soil.

## Hummingbird hawk
*Hemaris stellatarum*
SIZE AND DESCRIPTION
Forewing about 25 mm.
Mousy grey forewings and
hairy thorax. Hindwings golden
orange. Caterpillar, about 50 mm
long, is green with yellow, white and green
horizontal stripes.
HABITAT Parks, gardens across Southern Europe.
FOOD/HABITS Day-flying throughout the year.
Usually seen in summer in Britain. Hovers in
front of flowers drinking nectar through long
proboscis. Caterpillar feeds on bedstraws.

## White ermine
*Spilosoma lubricipeda*
SIZE AND DESCRIPTION Forewing
15–20 mm. White with more or
less sparse white spots. Hairy thorax
and yellow, black-spotted abdomen.
Larva up to 45 mm long, dark brown and
very hairy with dark red line down back.
HABITAT Hedgerows, gardens, waste ground
and other habitats throughout Europe.
FOOD/HABITS Flies May to August. Moth
does not feed, but larva feeds on
herbaceous plants, including docks,
dandelions and many garden plants.

### Garden tiger
*Arctia caja*

SIZE AND DESCRIPTION  Forewing 25–35 mm and chocolate-brown with cream patterning. Hindwings orange with black spots. Very hairy black and brown caterpillar known as a "woolly bear".

HABITAT  Open habitats including gardens and scrub throughout Europe.

FOOD/HABITS  Flies June to August. Caterpillar feeds on herbaceous plants. Winters as small caterpillar.

## Green arches
*Anaplectoides prasina*
SIZE AND DESCRIPTION
Forewing about 20 mm.
Greenish with variable
black markings. Hindwings
dark grey or brown. Larva
brown with darker markings.
HABITAT Deciduous woodland
over most of Europe.
FOOD/HABITS Flies at night from mid-June to mid-July. Larva
feeds on a variety of plants, especially honeysuckle and bilberry.

## Large yellow underwing
*Noctua pronuba*
SIZE AND DESCRIPTION
Forewing 25 mm and
varying from pale to dark
brown. Hindwings are deep
yellow with black border. The yellow
flashes when the moth takes to flight, which is thought to confuse predators.
Larva, up to 50 mm, is green with two rows of dark markings along back.
HABITAT Well-vegetated habitat across Europe except the far north.
FOOD/HABITS Flies from June to October. Fast erratic flight with noticeable
yellow flashes when flying, becoming invisible the moment it lands.

## Red underwing
*Catocala fraxini*

SIZE AND DESCRIPTION  Forewing 30–35 mm. Grey mottled forewings are well-camouflaged on tree-bark, but bright red underwing is very distinctive in flight. Pale brown caterpillar with warty, bud-like lumps on back.

HABITAT  Woodlands and gardens across Europe, except northern Scandinavia.

FOOD/HABITS  Flies in August, September. Larvae feed on willow, aspen and poplar.

## Angle shades
*Phlogophora meticulosa*

SIZE AND DESCRIPTION  Forewing about 25 mm. Varies from brown to green with distinctive v-shaped markings. Trailing edge of forewing has ragged appearance. Larva, up to 45 mm, fat and green with white line along back.

HABITAT  Common in Europe.

FOOD/HABITS  Flies May to October. Larvae feed on wild and cultivated plants. Overwinters as larva.

## Silver Y
*Autographa gamma*

SIZE AND DESCRIPTION  Forewing is about 20 mm. Varies from purple-tinged grey to almost black, with a silver y-mark on the forewing. Green larva, 25 mm long.

HABITAT  A migrant found all over Europe. Breeds all year in southern Europe. British and other northern breeders do not survive winter.

FOOD/HABITS  Flies throughout the year. Attracted by nectar.

## Common crane-fly or Daddy-long-legs
*Tipula paludosa*

SIZE AND DESCRIPTION About 25 mm long. Dark brown along the leading edges of wings. Wings of female are shorter than her abdomen. Male has square-ended abdomen, while female's is pointed with ovipositor. The dull brown grub is known as a "leatherjacket".

HABITAT Common in grasslands, parks and gardens across Europe.

FOOD/HABITS Flies throughout the year, but most numerous in autumn. Adults rarely feed. Grubs live in soil and appear at night to gnaw base of stems of plants.

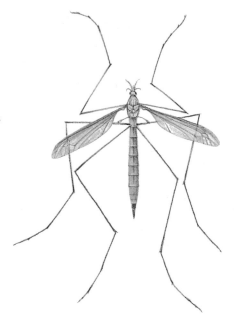

## Cleg-fly
*Haematopota pluvialis*

SIZE AND DESCRIPTION About 10 mm long. Dull grey with rather cylindrical abdomen. Wings are mottled. Holds wings above abdomen when at rest. Flies silently.

HABITAT Common from May to September, especially in damp woods.

FOOD/HABITS Flies from May to October. Often seen in thundery weather. Females are bloodsuckers, biting humans and livestock. Larvae live in soil.

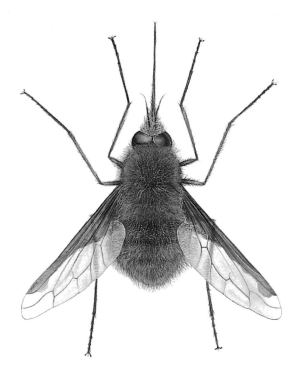

## Large bee-fly
*Bombylius major*

SIZE AND DESCRIPTION  10–12 mm. Brown furry, bee-like coat, but with long proboscis. Dark leading edge to wings. Long slender legs.

HABITAT  Found in wooded places across Europe, but rare further north.

FOOD/HABITS  Hovers, using long front legs to steady itself as it reaches nectar with its long proboscis. Larvae are parasitic on solitary bees and wasps.

### Drone-fly
*Eristalis tenax*
SIZE AND DESCRIPTION  10–15 mm long.
Looks like a honey bee drone. Dark anvil
marks on abdomen. Larva is a "rat-tailed"
maggot, with a long rear breathing tube.
HABITAT  Very common in gardens and
other flower-rich places across Europe.
FOOD/HABITS  Nectar and pollen. Can be
seen throughout the year. Larvae live in
stagnant water and dunghills.

### Syrphus-fly
*Syrphus ribesii*
SIZE AND DESCRIPTION  10 mm long. This hover-fly has a
yellow and black striped, rounded abdomen. Larva is
green and slug-like.
HABITAT  Flower-rich habitats across Europe.
FOOD/HABITS  Adults seen from March to November.
Males perch on leaves or twigs up to 2.5 m from the
ground. Feed mainly on nectar. Larvae feed on aphids
and is itself a victim of parasitic wasps.

### Narcissus-fly
*Merodon equestris*
SIZE AND DESCRIPTION  10–15 mm long.
Bumblebee mimic with black legs, with
prominent bulge on hind-legs and hairy
brownish-yellow abdomen.
HABITAT  Gardens, parks, wood and hedges
across Europe. Absent from far north.
FOOD/HABITS  Flies from March to August.
Larvae feed in daffodil and other bulbs.

### Common carrot-fly
*Psila rosae*
SIZE AND DESCRIPTION About 4 mm
long. Black thorax and abdomen with
brown eggs. Creamy white grub.
HABITAT Gardens and farmland.
FOOD/HABITS Lays eggs in late spring
near young carrots. Larvae infest the
roots, often turning them into
empty shells.

### Bluebottle
*Calliphora vomitoria*
SIZE AND DESCRIPTION 12–15 mm long.
Rounded metallic blue body. Creamy
white, carrot-shaped larva.
HABITAT Widespread through Europe.
Often seen in and around houses.
FOOD/HABITS Seen all year round, often
sunning on walls. Eggs are laid on meat
and carrion, on which larvae feed.

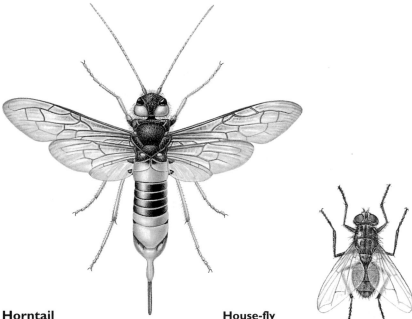

## Horntail
*Urceros gigas*
SIZE AND DESCRIPTION  Up to 40 mm long, including the ovipositor. Female is black and yellow. The male is smaller with an orange abdomen with a black tip and orange legs.
HABITAT  Coniferous woodland, but can survive in treated timber.
FOOD/HABITS  Female horntails are harmless. Fly in sunshine from May to October. Males usually fly near tree tops. Females drill into bark and deposit eggs in the trunk. Larvae are almost legless and feed on the timber.

## House-fly
*Musca domestica*
SIZE AND DESCRIPTION
8 mm long. Black and tan abdomen.
HABITAT  In and around houses throughout Europe. Especially numerous in places where there is plenty of decaying matter.
FOOD/HABITS  Found most of the year, but most common from June to September.

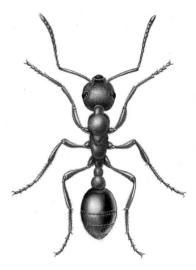

### Red ant
*Myrmica rubra*
SIZE AND DESCRIPTION Workers are 4–5 mm long. They are chestnut brown, with a pedicel of two segments. Males and queens, which appear in late summer and early autumn, are about one-and-a-half times as long as workers. Males have longer, less bulbous abdomens than females. Red ants can sting.
HABITAT Open habitats throughout Europe.
FOOD/HABITS Omnivorous, and, although less inclined towards honeydew than the black ant, it seems to prefer animal food. A colony contains one or more queens and a few hundred workers.

### Black garden ant
*Lasius niger*
SIZE AND DESCRIPTION Workers are up to 5 mm long. They are black or dark brown. Flying ants, which emerge in July and August, are males and females. They are about twice the size of workers. Does not sting.
HABITAT Open habitats including gardens throughout Europe.
FOOD/HABITS Feeds on anything, particularly if it is sweet. Is particularly fond of aphids which it "milks" for their honeydew. Winged males and females emerge for mating flights in summer. Some females survive to create new colonies.

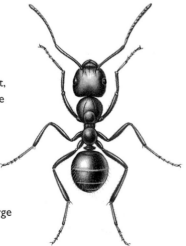

## German wasp
*Vespula germanica*
SIZE AND DESCRIPTION Worker is 12–16 mm long. Looks very like Common wasp, but marks on either side of the thorax bulge.
HABITAT Common in most habitats except northern Scandinavia.
FOOD/HABITS Nesting habits similar to Common wasp, but nest-paper is grayer and less brittle.

## Common wasp
*Vespula vulgaris*
SIZE AND DESCRIPTION Worker is 11–14 mm long. Black and yellow. Look for four yellow spots at the rear of the thorax. Yellow marks on either side of thorax usually have parallel sides.
HABITAT Common in most habitats across Europe.
FOOD/HABITS Usually nests in well-drained underground sites, such as hedgebanks, but will use cavities in walls and lofts. Nests are built of yellowish paper.

## Hornet
*Vespa crabro*

SIZE AND DESCRIPTION Worker is 20–30 mm long. Chestnut brown and yellow. Queens are much larger than any other wasps.
HABITAT Wooded areas, parks and gardens over most of Europe except Scotland, Ireland and northern Scandinavia.
FOOD/HABITS Nests in hollow trees, wall cavities and chimneys. Adults feed on the sap from damaged trunks. Preys on insects as large as butterflies and dragonflies to feed young. Less aggressive than common or German wasp.

### Tawny mining bee
*Andrena fulva*
SIZE AND DESCRIPTION 10–12 mm long.
Female has bright yellow abdomen,
while male's, which is smaller, is dark.
HABITAT Open habitats, in central and
southern Europe including southern
England.
FOOD/HABITS Flies from April to June.
Nests in the ground, especially on
lawns, throwing up soil in a small
volcano-like hole. Solitary species.

### Honey bee
*Apis mellifera*
SIZE AND DESCRIPTION 12–15 mm long.
Queens are about 20 mm long, but are
rarely seen outside the nest. Colours
vary from dark brown to orange. Can
be identified by narrow cell on leading
edge of the wing near the tip. Males
have stouter bodies.
HABITAT Worldwide.
FOOD/HABITS Flies from spring to late
autumn. Lives in colonies with a single
queen. Males or drones appear in
spring in small numbers. Nests contain
combs of hexagonal cells for rearing
grubs and storing pollen and honey.

### Buff-tailed bumble bee
*Bombus terrestris*

SIZE AND DESCRIPTION 20–22 mm long. Orange collar and second abdominal segment. The tip of the abdomen is buffish white. Tip of queen's abdomen is buffish in the British Isles, but white in continental Europe.

HABITAT Well-vegetated habitats across Europe except far north.

FOOD/HABITS Queens visit sallow catkins in March and April and workers often seen on apple and cherry blossom. Nests well below ground level.

### White-tailed bumble bee
*Bombus lucorum*

SIZE AND DESCRIPTION 20–22 mm long. Yellow collar and second abdominal segment with white tip to abdomen.

HABITAT Well-vegetated places throughout Europe.

FOOD/HABITS Very early flier with queens emerging in February and feeding on sallow catkins. Nests below ground.

### Garden bumble bee
*Bombus hortorum*

SIZE AND DESCRIPTION  20–24 mm long. Collar, rear of thorax and first segment of abdomen are yellow. Tip of the abdomen is whitish. Scruffy appearance.

HABITAT  Common in well-vegetated habitats, especially in gardens throughout Europe.

FOOD/HABITS  Queens often seen on white dead-nettle. Bees have a very long tongue which can be seen when feeding on long-necked flowers. Nests on or just beneath the ground.

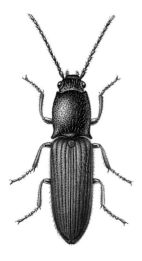

## Devil's coach horse

*Staphylinus olens*

SIZE AND DESCRIPTION  20–30 mm long.
Black with small, almost square elytra,
which leave the long abdomen
exposed.

HABITAT  Woods, hedges, parks and
gardens across Europe. Often found in
damp outhouses.

FOOD/HABITS  Nocturnal predator with
powerful jaws, feeding on slugs and
other invertebrates. When under
threat, the Devil's coach horse raises
its tail and opens its jaws.

## Click beetle

*Athous haemorrhoidalis*

SIZE AND DESCRIPTION  7–10 mm long.
Long, black or dark brown thorax and
brown ridged back. Larvae are brown
with thin, segmented body.

HABITAT  Grassland, including parks and
gardens across Europe except for
northern Scandinavia.

FOOD/HABITS  Fly from May to July.
Adults chew grasses and flowers,
especially stamens with pollen. Larvae
cause severe damage to roots. Flip
themselves into air when annoyed.

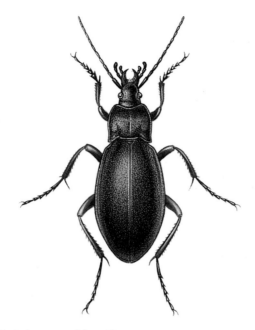

### Violet ground beetle
*Carabus violaceus*

SIZE AND DESCRIPTION  20–35 mm long. Although black all over, there are violet tinges to the thorax and elytra. The thorax is flanged and the elytra create a smooth oval shape. Larva has black head with segmented body.

HABITAT  Woods, hedges, gardens and scrub throughout Europe. Requires food, shelter and moisture.

FOOD/HABITS  Fast-running, non-flying predator on slugs and other invertebrates. Hides beneath stones and logs by day, emerging to hunt at night. Larva is also a predator, but less agile.

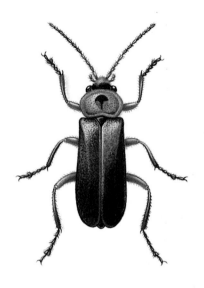

## Soldier beetle
*Cantharis rustica*
SIZE AND DESCRIPTION 11–14 mm long.
Black elytra with orange thorax with
dark mark. Beaded antennae.
HABITAT Abundant throughout Europe
in damp habitats, including woodland
edges and open country.
FOOD/HABITS Flies from May to August.
Preys on other insects. Found on
flower blooms.

## Cockchafer
*Melolontha melolontha*
SIZE AND DESCRIPTION 20–30 mm long.
Black thorax and rusty elytra which do
not quite cover the abdomen, exposing
a pointed tip. Legs are brown. Antennae
fan out. Males have larger antennae
than females. Larva is whitish with
brown head. It's smaller and wrinklier
than stag beetle.
HABITAT Throughout Europe, except
northern Scandinavia.
FOOD/HABITS Flies at night from May to
July. Adults chew leaves of trees and
shrubs. Larvae feed on roots.

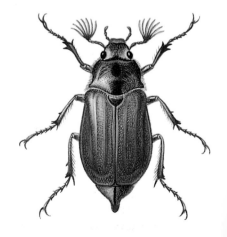

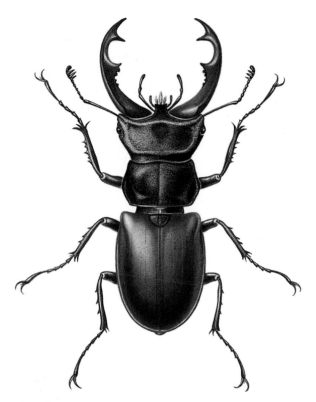

## Stag beetle
*Lucanus cervinus*

SIZE AND DESCRIPTION  25–75 mm long. Smooth, dark tan elytra and black head and thorax. Male has huge jaws which look like antlers (hence the name). Females lack the antlers. Whitish larva with brown head.

HABITAT  Oakwoods, parkland and gardens in southern and central Europe, including England. Becoming increasingly rare.

FOOD/HABITS  Flies from May to August at night. Feeds on sap. Larvae feed in rotten wood. Males battle with "antlers" in the breeding season.

## Seven-spot ladybird
*Coccinella 7-punctata*
SIZE AND DESCRIPTION 5.2–8 mm long.
Bright red elytra with seven black
spots. Larvae are steely blue with
yellow or cream spots.
HABITAT Well-vegetated habitats
throughout Europe. Abundant.
FOOD/HABITS Flies from early spring to
autumn. Adults and larvae feed on
aphids. Winter is passed in small groups
or individually in leaf litter and
sheltered places.

## Two-spot ladybird
*Adalia bipunctata*
SIZE AND DESCRIPTION 3.5–5.5 mm long.
Colour varies, northern populations
often being largely black. The most
common form is red with a bold black
spot on each elytron. Larvae are similar
to seven-spot ladybird.
HABITAT Well-vegetated habitats across
Europe. Abundant.
FOOD/HABITS Flies from spring to
autumn and feeds on aphids. Winters in
groups, sometimes in thousands, in
sheds and houses. Sites are used by
successive generations.

## Pea weevil
*Sitona lineatus*
SIZE AND DESCRIPTION  4–5 mm long. Pale and dark brown stripes run along its body. Eyes are prominent.
HABITAT  Found wherever wild and cultivated leguminous plants grow. Absent from northern Scandinavia.
FOOD/HABITS  Adults, which are mainly active in spring and autumn, chew semi-circular pieces from the edges of leaves and may damage seedlings. Larvae live inside root nodules. Several species of weevil attack garden plants.

## Yellow ophion
*Ophion luteus*
SIZE AND DESCRIPTION  15–20 mm. Yellowish brown, strongly arched abdomen and thorax. Large eyes.
HABITAT  Well-vegetated habitats throughout most Europe except the far north.
FOOD/HABITS  Adults fly from July to October. Attracted by lighted windows and feeding on nectar and pollen. Eggs are laid in caterpillars or pupae of several species. There is usually one grub per host. The adult always emerges from the host's pupa.

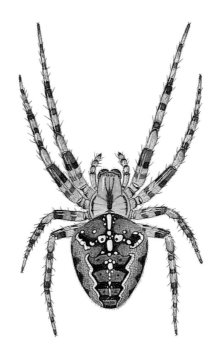

## Garden spider
*Araneus diadematus*

SIZE AND DESCRIPTION  Female 10–13 mm long. Male 4–8 mm. White
cross on abdomen. Male has smaller abdomen. Colours vary from
pale yellowish-brown to very dark brown.

HABITAT  Common in gardens, hedges, woodland and heathland
throughout northern Europe.

FOOD/HABITS  Web-spinner, which preys on flies and other insects.
Female protects an egg-sac with which she remains until her death.

## House spider

*Tegenaria duellica*

SIZE AND DESCRIPTION 11–16 mm long. Colour is dark brown, with pale markings. The male is smaller than the female, but has longer legs.

HABITAT Widespread in northern Europe near human habitation.

FOOD/HABITS May be seen running across floors at night, especially in autumn, when males are seeking mates. Builds a triangular web.

## Nursery-web spider

*Pisaura mirabilis*

SIZE AND DESCRIPTION 10–15 mm long. Sexes are similar, but males are smaller, with narrower abdomens. Colours vary from yellow to brown, with markings that may be very clear or even absent.

HABITAT Widespread across northern Europe.

FOOD/HABITS Seen in summer. Diurnal hunter. Female carries her egg-cocoon with her fangs. Spins a silken tent over it and guards it until the young leave.

## Common newt
*Triturus vulgaris*

SIZE AND DESCRIPTION  Length 7–11 cm. In the breeding season, the male develops a wavy crest from the neck to the tip of its tail. Each wave is topped by a black mark. The bright orange belly has black spots. Females are smaller, less clearly marked, lack the crest and have paler bellies.

HABITAT  Lives in damp places in a range of habitats across Europe. Not in southern Europe and northern Scandinavia.

FOOD/HABITS  Insects, caterpillars, worms and slugs are the main diet on land, while in the water, insects, crustaceans, molluscs and tadpoles are eaten. Adults come out of hibernation in February/March. They leave the water in June/July, hibernating again in October.

## Common toad
*Bufo bufo*

SIZE AND DESCRIPTION 8–15 cm long. Females are larger than males. The skin is warty and of varying colour, but usually orange-brown or olive. Walks and hops.

HABITAT Absent from Ireland, northern Scandinavia and Mediterranean islands. Lives in a wide range of habitats, but is usually found in damp places.

FOOD/HABITS Insects, larvae, spiders, worms and slugs form most of the toad's diet. Prey is grabbed by the long, sticky, prehensile tongue. Toads emerge from hibernation in mild weather during February/March to enter the water. Adults leave the water after spawning and hibernate in October.

## Common frog
*Rana temporaria*

SIZE AND DESCRIPTION  6–8 cm long. Differs from common toad by its
smooth skin and longer hindlegs. The hindlegs are short compared
with other frog species. Colour and pattern vary. The snout is
rounded and the large black eyes are surrounded by gold, flecked
with brown. Moves with a springing leap.

HABITAT  Widespread in moist, shady habitats across Europe, from
northern Spain to the North Cape, but absent from Iceland, Orkney
and Shetland.

FOOD/HABITS  Snails, slugs, worms, beetles, woodlice and flies are all
flicked into the frog's wide mouth by its long tongue. Frogs hibernate
in pond mud or rotting vegetation on land.

## Viviparous lizard
*Lacerta vivipara*

SIZE AND DESCRIPTION Total length is 10–16 cm. The tail is up to twice the length of the body. The head is small, the neck thick, and the skin has obvious scales and a variable pattern. Females usually have a stripe down the middle of the back. The pale spots on the back are more obvious on the male, while the pale underside may be orange in some males.

HABITAT Occurs across Europe. The only lizard in northern Norway.

FOOD/HABITS Hunts during the day, using sight and scent. Prey include spiders, insects and small snails. Hibernation is from October to March.

## Common wall lizard
*Podarcis muralis*

SIZE AND DESCRIPTION Total length is 18–20 cm. The tail can be more than twice the length of the body. Head is longer and more pointed than the viviparous lizard's. Colours vary from brownish, greyish-green.

HABITAT Northern Spain across France and Italy to the Balkans and Greece.

FOOD/HABITS These lizards feed on small invertebrates. Hibernation is from November to February.

## Grass snake

*Natrix natrix*

SIZE AND DESCRIPTION  70–150 cm long. Females are bigger than males. This slender snake has a distinct head and is typically coloured pale, with dark marks on either side of the neck. The mouth looks curved. The viperine snake of France and Spain looks very similar.

HABITAT  Lowland hedgerows, woodland margins, heaths, moorland, water-meadows, gravel pits and gardens. From England and Wales across Europe, north from Spain to southern Scandinavia and Russia.

FOOD/HABITS  Frogs, fish, tadpoles, newts, fish, mice, voles and birds are all hunted. The grass snake swims well. It hibernates from October to March in holes, crevices and manure heaps.

## Collared dove
*Streptopelia decaocto*

SIZE AND DESCRIPTION  31–33 cm long. Slimmer than other pigeons. The back is brown buff, while the head and underparts are pinkish-brown. There is a distinctive black ring around the neck.

VOICE  A rapidly repeated "koo-koo, koo" call.

HABITAT  Towns, gardens and farmland with hedges. Has spread across Europe from Asia.

FOOD/HABITS  Feeds on seeds and grain. A frequent bird-table visitor. Large flocks assemble at grain stores.

juvenile

## Wood pigeon
*Columba palumbus*

SIZE AND DESCRIPTION Measuring 40–42 cm long, this is the largest of the European pigeons. Adults have white rings around the neck, and a white bar across each wing. The wings make a clattering sound on take-off and landing. The body is noticeably large in flight.

VOICE A soft, often repeated "coo-coo-coo-cu-coo".

HABITAT Common across Europe, but not Iceland and the far north.

FOOD/HABITS Eats seeds, berries and beechmast. Feeds in flocks throughout the winter.

## Feral pigeon
*Columba livia*

SIZE AND DESCRIPTION 31–33 cm long. With black wing-bars and a white rump, many feral pigeons resemble the rock doves from which they originate. But colours may vary from white to very dark grey, and some may be pale fawn.

VOICE A soft cooing.

HABITAT Sea cliffs, towns and villages.

FOOD/HABITS Seeds, grain and discarded human food.

## Great spotted woodpecker
*Dendrocops major*

SIZE AND DESCRIPTION  23–26 cm long.
A blackbird-sized, black-and-white
bird. It has white shoulder patches,
with red under the tail. The male has a
red patch on the nape, while the
female's nape is black. Juvenile has a red
crown. Flight is undulating. Similar species
include the lesser spotted woodpecker,
which is sparrow-sized.

VOICE  A short, sharp "tchak" call, which
may be repeated at 1-second intervals.
In spring, it drums very fast on rotten branches.

HABITAT  All kinds of woodland, large gardens and parks.

FOOD/HABITS  Insects, grubs and conifer seeds in winter. Will visit
garden feeders. Also steals eggs and young from other birds' nests.

## House martin
*Delichon urbica*

SIZE AND DESCRIPTION 12.5 cm long. Wings are broader than the swallow's and the forked tail is shorter. The rump is white, while the wings, head and tail are dark blue. Flight is more fluttery than the swallow's.
VOICE A harsh twitter, becoming higher and more drawn-out when agitated.
HABITAT Breeds in colonies in towns and villages.
FOOD/HABITS Feeds on flying insects. Rarely touches ground, except to collect mud for its nest.

## Swift
*Apus apus*

SIZE AND DESCRIPTION 17 cm long. The swift has long, narrow, crescent-shaped wings, a torpedo-shaped body and a short forked tail. It has a dark brown plumage with a pale throat.
VOICE A shrill, monotone scream, which is often uttered by tight flocks flying around buildings.
HABITAT Breeds in towns and villages. A summer visitor to northern Europe (except Iceland), usually arriving in May and leaving in August.
FOOD/HABITS The swift is adapted to feed on high-flying insects, which it catches in its wide, gaping mouth.

juvenile

## Swallow
*Hirundo rustica*

SIZE AND DESCRIPTION 17–22 cm long, including a tail of 3–6.5 cm. The swallow's wings are long and pointed, and its tail deeply forked. It has pale cream underparts, dark blue wings and back, and a red throat with a blue-black neck band. Flight is fast, with powerful wingbeats.

VOICE In flight, it has a high-pitched "vit-vit" call. The warning call for cats (and other ground predators) is a sharp "sifflit"; for birds of prey it is a "flitt-flitt". The song is a rapid, rattling twitter.

HABITAT Breeds in farmyards and small-village gardens with surrounding open country. Often seen near water. It is a summer visitor to northern Europe, arriving in late March and April, and leaving in September and October. On migration, swallows roost in flocks in reedbeds and scrub.

FOOD/HABITS Feeds on insects, which it catches in flight by flying low over fields and water, maneouvring to avoid obstacles.

pied wagtail

white wagtail

## Pied/White wagtail
*Moticilla alba*

SIZE AND DESCRIPTION 17–19 cm long. The male of the British race, has a black back and wings, and the female a dark grey back; in the continental race, the white wagtail, both male and female have a pale grey back. In flight, which is undulating, faint double wing bars can be seen. On the ground, the gait is rapid, with the head moving back and forth and the tail wagging – hence the name.

VOICE Typcal flight call is a "chissick", sometimes a "chissick-ick". Song is plain and twittery.

HABITAT Towns, gardens and open habitat, usually near water. In winter, although feeding singly or in small flocks, pied wagtails roost in large flocks in warm places, such as around factories and town centres.

FOOD/HABITS Runs rapidly after flying insects, sometimes snatching them with a small leap into the air. Prefers feeding on lawns, roofs, car parks and roads.

# Wren
*Troglodytes troglodytes*
SIZE AND DESCRIPTION 9–10 cm long. The wren looks rather mouse-like on occasions. Its reddish-brown back is faintly barred, as are the paler flanks. There is a narrow dark eye-stripe, with a paler stripe above the eye. The bill is narrow, pointed and slightly downward-curving. The wren has a whirring flight.

VOICE Calls are a repeated "tic-tic" and a metallic "clink". The song is a surprisingly loud series of trills and warbles, delivered from prominent song-posts.

HABITAT Woodland with dense undergrowth, scrub, gardens and moorland.

FOOD/HABITS Searches for insects and spiders on or near the ground, moving in a rather mouse-like way. In winter, flocks of wrens will roost together, in a bundle on cold nights.

## Mistle thrush
*Turdus viscivorus*

SIZE AND DESCRIPTION  22–27 cm long. This largish thrush has a comparatively longer tail than the song thrush. Its white breast is speckled with rounded, blotchy spots. In flight, the white outer tail feathers and narrow white wing-bars can be seen. The underwing is white. On the ground, stands in an upright posture. Flight is more undulating than the song thrush's.

VOICE  Its flight call is a dry, churring rattle. Song is full-blooded, but similar in form to the song thrush's. It is often performed in bad weather, such as rain, when other birds are not singing.

HABITAT  Breeds in open woodland, orchards, parks and gardens. Moves to fields to feed in winter.

FOOD/HABITS  Eats worms, berries and insects. Less likely to be seen in flocks than most thrushes, but will feed alongside other species. May be seen in family flocks of about half a dozen birds.

## Song thrush
*Turdus philomelos*

SIZE AND DESCRIPTION  20–22 cm long. The song thrush has a brown back and a speckled creamy breast (speckles are shaped like arrowheads, and more regular than those of the mistle thrush). Shortish brown tail is not as short as the starling's. The underwing shows yellowish-orange. Flies rather jerkily.

VOICE  A loud, strong song, with a variety of trilling and squeaky notes with few pauses and frequent repetitions. The alarm call is a series of sharp notes.

HABITAT  Woodlands and gardens. Seriously in decline in Britain.

FOOD/HABITS  Feeds on worms, insects, berries and snails.

## Dunnock
*Prunella modularis*

SIZE AND DESCRIPTION  13–15 cm long. The streaking and brown colour of the dunnock give it a rather sparrow-like appearance, which is why it is often wrongly described as a hedge sparrow. Has a thin insect-picking bill, grey throat and face, and reddish-brown legs.

VOICE  The alarm-call is a strong "tiih". The song is clear and quite loud, but not as sweet or as focused as the robin's.

HABITAT  Gardens, parks, open woodland, heathland, farmland hedges. Resident over most of Europe.

FOOD/HABITS  Searches on the ground for seeds, berries, insects and other invertebrates.

## Blackbird
*Turdus merula*

SIZE AND DESCRIPTION  23.5–29 cm long. The all-black male, with its yellow bill and yellow eye-ring, is unmistakable. The sooty-brown female, with a dark-streaked pale throat, and the gingery juveniles may be confused with other thrushes, but they have a solid build and cock their tails when landing. First-winter males have all-dark bills.

VOICE  Alarm call is a harsh "chack-aack-aack-aack", or a series of high metallic notes when going to roost or when a cat is seen. The song is a rich, melodic fluting, often rising to a crescendo.

HABITAT  Woodland, parks, orchards and gardens across Europe. Blackbirds in eastern Europe and Scandinavia migrate in winter.

FOOD/HABITS  Hops or walks over the ground, stopping and cocking its head to look for worms or other food. Takes a wide range of food, including insects, worms, fruit and berries.

# Robin

*Erithacus rubecula*

SIZE AND DESCRIPTION   12.5–14 cm. Adopts a perky stance. The orange-red breast is fringed with pale grey. Underparts are pale and the back brown. The head seems rather large and the legs are comparatively long and thin. There is a pale wing-bar. Juvenile has a pale-spotted brown breast, and a pale-flecked head and back, with the wing-bar quite noticeable.

VOICE   The call is a short, hard repeated "tic", repeated most rapidly when anxious and going to roost. The alarm call is a thin, sharp "tsiih".

HABITAT   A woodland bird that breeds in gardens, parks and forest edges.

FOOD/HABITS   Feeds on berries and insects on the ground. Moves over the ground by hopping vigorously. In winter, the robin will search for food in mole-hills, animal tracks in the snow and where soil is being turned over by gardeners.

## Goldcrest
*Regulus regulus*

SIZE AND DESCRIPTION 8.5–9.5 cm long. This tiny bird has a greenish back, and a yellow crest that becomes orange in the male. The crest has a black stripe on each side. The face is greyish, with dark eyes surrounded by very pale grey.

VOICE A very high-pitched, thin call of three or four syllables: "see-see-see". Song is high-pitched and rhythmic, ending with a trill.

HABITAT Coniferous and mixed woodlands, spruce and fir preferred. In gardens, goldcrests are often seen in yew and cypress trees.

FOOD/HABITS Eats tiny insects and spiders. In winter, it will join flocks of tits.

## Spotted flycatcher
*Muscicapa striata*

SIZE AND DESCRIPTION 13.5–15 cm long. Greyish brown back and pale underparts, close examination reveals its streaked forehead and faintly streaked upper breast. Its bill and legs are black, and has a black eye. When perched, its posture is upright.

VOICE The call is a short, shrill "tzee". The song is quiet, simple and scratchy.

HABITAT Open woodland, parks and gardens.

FOOD/HABITS Snatches insect in flight and then returns to the same perch.

## Blue tit

*Parus caeruleus*

SIZE AND DESCRIPTION  11–12 cm long. Smaller than the great tit and possessing a bright blue crown. The stripe down the yellow breast is less well-defined than the great tit's. The tail and wings are blue. Young birds have yellow cheeks, and the blue parts are green.

VOICE  A clear, ringing, high-pitched song, and a thin "see-see" call.

HABITAT  Mixed and deciduous woodlands, parks and gardens. Found across Europe, except in Iceland and northern Norway.

FOOD/HABITS  Feeds on insects, spiders and other small animals, finding them on branches and sometimes in the corners of windows. Often visits the bird table in winter. Feeds in flocks of up to 30 in winter, often with other species of tit.

## Great tit
*Parus major*

SIZE AND DESCRIPTION  14 cm long. A black cap and a black stripe starting at the bill give the great tit a more ferocious expression than the blue tit. The male's breast-stripe becomes broader than the female's, and his colours tend to be more intense. Young birds have yellow cheeks for a few weeks.

VOICE  The great tit's rich and varied repertoire includes a metallic "pink" and a repeated "teacher-teacher".

HABITAT  Woodlands and gardens. Many of the tits feeding in gardens in winter return to woods to feed in spring. Found across Europe, except in northern Norway.

FOOD/HABITS  Feeds on seeds and fruits. Also takes spiders and insect larvae. Eats sunflower seeds, peanuts, and fat at bird-tables. Feeds on the ground and in trees.

## Long-tailed tit
*Aegithalos caudatus*
SIZE AND DESCRIPTION 12–14 cm long,
including a tail that is at least as long as
the dumpy body. With its pink, black
and white body and long tail, the
long-tailed tit is unmistakable.
VOICE High-pitched piercing, trisyllabic call.
HABITAT Woods with bushy undergrowth, hedges
and gardens.
FOOD/HABITS Feeds mainly on insects and small spiders, will visit bird-
tables. Families form into flocks and move through woods and hedges,
with other tits.

## Coal tit
*Parus ater*

SIZE AND DESCRIPTION  11.5 cm long. Smaller than the great tit, with a proportionately larger head. Black head has white cheeks, and there is a white patch on the nape. The back is grey and the breast is grey-brown. The double wing-bar shows in flight.

VOICE  Call is a triple "tsee-tsee-tsee". The song is like a simpler, weaker great tit's song.

HABITAT  Woodlands and gardens. Prefers coniferous trees.

FOOD/HABITS  Eats insects and seeds, particularly spruce cones.

## Nuthatch
*Sitta europaea*

SIZE AND DESCRIPTION  12–14.5 cm. The large head, lack of neck, short tail and heavy pointed bill give this sparrow-sized bird a distinctive shape. The back and head are slate-grey, with a long black eye-stripe. The cheeks are white and the breast and underparts are rusty orange (darker in the male than in the female). Flight is undulating like a woodpecker's, tail-shape is rounded.

VOICE  A loud, strident "hwitt" call . The song is a repetitive "peeu-peeu-peeu".

HABITAT  Mixed and deciduous woods, and in parks and gardens. Across Europe.

FOOD/HABITS  Eats nuts, seeds and invertebrates. Often descends trees head first.

## Magpie
*Pica pica*

SIZE AND DESCRIPTION  40–51 cm long, of which 20–30 cm is the tail. Wings are a metallic blue-black and the long, round-tipped tail has a metallic green sheen. Males are larger and tend to have longer tails than the females. Flight is often a series of flaps interspersed with swooping glides. It walks with a strong gait, holding its tail well above the ground.

VOICE  The magpie's noisy alarm call is a staccato, rather machine-gun-like rattle. Other magpie sounds include a variety of bisyllabic calls.

HABITAT  Breeds around farms and villages and in hedgerows. It is becoming increasingly common in urban areas. The magpie occurs throughout Europe, except in Iceland, northernmost Scotland and the far north of Norway.

FOOD/HABITS  The magpie is an omnivore that feeds on seeds, insects, nestlings, eggs and carrion (it is often seen feeding on roadside casualties). It sometimes gathers in flocks of up to 25 birds.

## Carrion/hooded crow

*Corvus corone*

SIZE AND DESCRIPTION   44–51 cm long. The carrion crow is totally black, with a stout bill. The hooded crow, the subspecies found in northern Europe, has grey underparts and a grey back. In flight, the wingbeats are shallow, the tail is rounded and the wings are uniformly broad.

VOICE   A hard, rolling "krra-kra-kraa" is the commonest call.

HABITAT   The carrion/hooded crow is found in a wide variety of habitats, from the coast to the mountains, including towns, parks and large gardens. The carrion crow is found in England, Wales and Scotland (except in the far north) and on the continent from Germany to Portugal. The hooded crow is found in Ireland, the far north of Scotland and Europe east of Germany.

FOOD/HABITS   An omnivore, this crow feeds on carrion, nestlings and eggs, grain and insects. It is less sociable than the rook, but may still be seen in flocks.

## Jackdaw
*Corvus monedula*

SIZE AND DESCRIPTION 30–34 cm long. Its nape is grey and its eye has a very pale iris. On the ground, its stance is more upright than the carrion crow, and it struts as it walks. The wings appear longer and narrower in proportion to the body, and the small bill makes the head look smaller.

VOICE Common calls are a metallic, high-pitched "kya" and "chak".

HABITAT Most of Europe, except far north. Open woodland and farmland.

FOOD/HABITS Eats invertebrates, such as worms, insect larvae, eggs and nestlings of other birds, small mammals and grain.

## Starling
*Sturnus vulgaris*

SIZE AND DESCRIPTION 19–22 cm long. It has a short tail and neck, an upright stance, pink legs, white spots and a metallic green shine. Tends to be seen in flocks. In flight, the short tail and pointed wings give the bird an arrowhead profile. Flocks fly in tight formation. Swirling flocks of thousands of birds gather at winter roosts. Juveniles are grey brown.

VOICE Mimics of other birds, but its own calls are chirps, clicks and whistles.

HABITAT Found across Europe in almost all habitats.

FOOD/HABITS Starlings eat a wide variety of food. In winter, large flocks forage in fields and gardens, as well as on the seashore. Outside breeding season, roosts in huge flocks.

## Chiffchaff
*Phylloscopus collybita*

SIZE AND DESCRIPTION 10–12 cm long. A small, neat bird, with a fine bill and thin legs. Very similar to willow warbler. The legs are usually dark and the bill is even finer than the willow warbler's. The stripe above the eye is less distinct and shorter, while the darkish patch beneath the eye emphasises the white eye-ring. The primary feathers do not project very far beyond the tertial feathers. The chiffchaff's habit of flicking its tail downwards is characteristic.

VOICE The call is a soft "hueet", and the song is a distinctively slow and measured "chiff-chaff-chiff-chaff".

HABITAT Usually breeds in open deciduous woodland with some scrub. Mainly a summer visitor to the British Isles, Scandinavia and central Europe, arriving in mid-March. Most likely to be seen in gardens while in transit.

FOOD/HABITS Feeds on small insects, which it finds by flitting among foliage. Eats berries in autumn.

## House sparrow
*Passer domesticus*
SIZE AND DESCRIPTION  14–16 cm
long. The male has a grey cap and
grey breast, with an extensive
black throat-patch. The
brown back has dark
streaks in both sexes. The
female has a pale brown cap
and buff eye-stripe. The wings of both sexes have small white wing-bars.
VOICE  A number of monotonous chirps.
HABITAT  It is found in towns, villages and farmland near human habitation.
In winter, flocks can be seen feeding in fields. Found across Europe except
northern Norway, wherever there is a human presence.
FOOD/HABITS  Feeds on seeds and insects, as well as bread and other food
left by people. Social, even when breeding.

## Greenfinch
*Carduelis chloris*

SIZE AND DESCRIPTION 14–16 cm long.
The greenfinch is stouter than most other
finches. In summer, adults are olive-green,
merging into grey-green on the face, wings and
flanks, with bright yellow wing feathers on
either side of the tail. The female's colouring is subdued, with faint brownish streaks
on the back; juvenile is paler and even more streaked. Flight is bouncing and undulating.
VOICE Flight call is a sharp "burrurrup", while the song is a wheezy sequence of
twitters and whistles.
HABITAT Woodland edges, parks, gardens and farmland with hedges. In winter,
flocks may be seen feeding in farmland and gardens. All of Europe, except far north.
FOOD/HABITS Seeds and berries, along with some insects during the breeding
season. A visitor to garden bird-tables.

## Hedgehog
*Erinaceus europaeus*

SIZE AND DESCRIPTION Body is 20–30 cm long; tail measures 1–4 cm. The rounded, rather short body is covered with spines, which are dark with creamy tips. The face and undersides are covered with coarse hairs. The hedgehog has longish legs, and each foot has five long toes. Its nose is pointed, the ears and eyes are small, and the teeth are pointed.

HABITAT Found from lowlands up to 2,000 m, where there is ground cover for shelter and nesting. Occurs across Europe, from south Scandinavia and Finland.

FOOD/HABITS Usually nocturnal, the hedgehog finds prey by sound and scent. It eats invertebrates, including slugs, worms and beetles, as well as bird eggs, nestlings and carrion. It runs quite swiftly, can climb banks, and can also swim. Foxes and badgers often eat them. Cars, lawn-mowers and poisoning by chemicals, such as slug pellets, are the main causes of death. Hibernation begins in October, and ends in March or April.

## Mole

*Talpa europaea*

SIZE AND DESCRIPTION  Body is 11–16 cm long; tail measures 2–4 cm. With its soft grey-black fur, cylindrical shape, massive earth-moving front paws and pink, bewhiskered nose, the mole is very distinctive. Its tiny eyes are covered by fur. The mole is rarely seen above ground.

HABITAT  This woodland species has adapted to fields, parks and gardens. It is absent from Iceland, Ireland, south-west Spain, Greece, much of Italy, Norway and northern Sweden.

FOOD/HABITS  Three- or four-hour sessions of activity alternate with similar periods of rest and sleep. The mole's tunnels may be 1 metre deep and 200 m long. Food is earthworms and insect larvae, found by smell and hearing. Cats, dogs, tawny owls, stoats, and keen gardeners are the mole's main enemies.

## Wood mouse
*Apodemus sylvaticus*
SIZE AND DESCRIPTION
Body is 8–10 cm
long; tail measures
6.9–11.5 cm. Fur is
orange-brown, large ears
and a tail that may be longer
than its body. Underparts are pale grey.
HABITAT Found in every habitat, except those
that are too wet or above 2,500 m. Distributed
across Europe, including Iceland but excluding
much of Norway, Sweden and all of Finland.
FOOD/HABITS Forages largely at night for seeds, buds, fruits, nuts, snails
and spiders. A good climber, it can be found in trees and will enter houses
in search of food. It does not hibernate, but slows down in cold weather.

## House mouse
*Mus domesticus*
SIZE AND DESCRIPTION
Body is 7–10 cm long;
tail measures
6.5–10 cm.
Uniformly
greyish fur,
with a thick,
scaly tail. Colour
varies. A strong
musky smell is emitted when they are disturbed.
HABITAT Found in buildings and on farmland throughout Europe.
FOOD/HABITS Primarily a grain-eater, the house mouse feeds on a
wide variety of seeds, roots, fungi, and invertebrates.

### Grey squirrel
*Sciurus carolinensis*

SIZE AND DESCRIPTION  Body is 23–30 cm long; tail measures 19–24 cm. The grey fur is variably tinged with red and yellow. Some individuals can be noticeably red in summer. The rounded ears are never tufted.

HABITAT  The grey squirrel is a north American species that has been introduced to Britain and Ireland, where it is now very common. Spreading to mainland Europe.

FOOD/HABITS  The squirrel is active during the day, with peak activity occurring four or five hours after dawn. In summer, foraging takes place mainly in trees, but it will also search on the ground for fungi, bulbs, roots and cached acorns and other nuts. Food includes eggs, nestlings, leaves, buds and shoots. The drey is a large structure of twigs, leaves, bark and grass, in which the squirrel shelters from severe weather. It does not hibernate, and can only survive three days without feeding.

## Red squirrel
*Sciurus vulgaris*
SIZE AND DESCRIPTION  Body is
up to 25 cm long; tail measures
up to 20 cm. Two colour phases
exist on the continent: dark greyish-
brown and russet red. Only the red phase is found in the British Isles. In winter, the
fur becomes greyer and the ear-tufts are prominent. In the British subspecies, the
tail can be very pale in summer. Smaller than the grey squirrel.
HABITAT  Forests, especially coniferous ones. Found up to 2,000 m in the Alps and
Pyrenees. Distributed across Europe from northern Spain to northern Russia.
Restricted mainly to Scotland and Ireland in the British Isles.
FOOD/HABITS  A solitary, diurnal animal, with peaks of activity around dawn and dusk.
Feeds high in the canopy on seeds in cones, berries and fruit. Will eat insects,
nestling birds and eggs. Hoards food.

## Pipistrelle
*Pipistrellus pipistrellus*

SIZE AND DESCRIPTION  Body is 3.5–4.9 cm long; wingspan is 27–30 cm. A very small bat, the pipistrelle has a soft reddish coat, but colours may vary. The rounded head has small triangular ears. In flight, the wings are narrow. Fast and jerky flight.

HABITAT  Found across Europe, in all but the most exposed habitats. Absent from Iceland and southernmost parts of Scandinavia.

FOOD/HABITS  In summer, pipistrelles roost in buildings. In winter, they use both buildings and natural sites for hibernation. Roosts are indicated by a pile of cylindrical droppings about 0.5 cm long.

### Edible dormouse
*Glis glis*

SIZE AND DESCRIPTION  Body is 13–19 cm long; tail measures 11–15 cm. Uniformly grey, with a faint yellowish tinge, the edible dormouse has a fleshy nose and naked, rounded ears and large eyes.

HABITAT  Mature woodlands, parks and large gardens. Distributed across Europe but absent from Scandinavia.

FOOD/HABITS  Nocturnal and secretive. It forages in the tree canopy, but will enter sheds and lofts in search of food. Nuts, berries, insects, nestlings and eggs are eaten.

## Red fox
*Vulpes vulpes*

SIZE AND DESCRIPTION  Body is 56–77 cm long; tail measures 28–49 cm; height at shoulder is 35–40 cm. The pointed nose, pointed ears and bushy tail make this reddish-brown animal, which is the size of a large domestic cat, unmistakable. Males weigh about 15% more than females.

HABITAT  If there is sufficient cover, red foxes will be found in every type of habitat up to 3,500 m. Widespread across Europe, absent from Iceland. They are now found in parks, gardens and industrial areas of cities.

FOOD/HABITS  Active mostly at night, with peak activity at dawn and dusk, the fox preys on rabbits, hares, rats, voles and ground-nesting birds, including domestic hens and ducks. About two-thirds of an urban fox's diet is human refuse. It also feeds on carrion. Earthworms are an important food for cubs. Hedgerow berries and fruit are also eaten. Foxes live in family groups, made up of a dog fox, a dominant vixen and up to six other females.

# Addresses

Bat Conservation Trust
15 Cloisters House
8 Battersea Park Road
London SW8 4BG
Tel  020 7627 2629
Fax 020 7627 2628
E-mail  Enquiries@bats.org.uk
Website  www.bats.org.uk

British Trust for Ornithology
The Nunnery
Thetford
Norfolk IP24 2PU
Tel  01842 750050
Fax 01842 750030
E-mail  info@bto.org
Website  www.bto.org

RSPB
The Lodge
Sandy
Bedfordshire SG19 2DL
Tel  01767 680551
Fax 01767 692365
E-mail  bird@rspb.demon.co.uk
Website  www.rspb.org.uk

Plantlife
21 Elizabeth Street
London SW1W 9RP
Tel  020 7808 0100
Fax 020 7730 8377
E-mail  enquiries@plantlife.org.uk
Website  www.plantlife.org.uk

The Wildlife Trusts
The Kiln
Waterside
Mather Road
Newark
Nottinghamshire NG24 1WT
Tel  0870 036 7711
Fax 0870 036 0101
E-mail  info@wildlife-trusts.cix.co.uk
Website  www.wildlifetrusts.org

Wildlife Watch
(Contact details as above)
E-mail watch@wildlife-trusts.cix.co.uk

Birdguides
Videos, CDs, CD-Roms
Tel  0800 919391
Website  www.birdguides.com

NHBS
2-3 Wills Road
Totnes
Devon TQ9 5XN
Tel  01803 865913
E-mail  nhbs@nhbs.co.uk
Website  www.nhbs.com

# Suggested reading

Arnold, E. N., Burton, J. A. & Ovenden, D.
*Field Guide to Reptiles and Amphibians of Britain and Europe*
Collins, 1978

Carter, D. & Hargreaves, B.
*A Field Guide to the Caterpillars of Butterflies and Moths in Britain and Europe*
Collins, 1986

Chinery, Michael
*Butterflies of Britain and Europe*
Collins and The Wildlife Trusts, 1998

Chinery, Michael
*New Generation Guide to Butterflies and Day-flying Moths of Britain and Europe*
Collins, 1989

Chinery, Michael
*Collins Guide to the Insects of Britain and Western Europe*
Collins, 1986

Golley, M., Moss, S. & Daly, D.
*The Complete Garden Bird Book*
New Holland, 1998

Jonsson, Lars
*Birds of Europe*
Helm, 1992

Macdonald, D. & Barrett, P.
*Field Guide to Mammals of Britain and Europe*
Collins, 1993

Moss, Stephen & Cottridge, David
*Attracting Birds to Your Garden*
New Holland, 1997

Mullarney, K., Svensson, K., Zetterstrom, D. & Grant, P.
*Collins Field Guide to the Birds of Britain & Europe*
Harper Collins, 1999

Oxford, R.
*Minibeast Magic – Kind Hearted Capture Techniques for Invertebrates*
Yorkshire Wildlife Trust, 1999

Packham, Chris
*Chris Packham's Back Garden Nature Reserve*
New Holland & The Wildlife Trusts, 2001

Powell, Dan
*A Guide to the Dragonflies of Great Britain*
Arlequin, 1999

Roberts, Michael J.
*Field Guide to Spiders of Britain and Northern Europe*
Collins, 1995

Skinner, B.
*Colour Identification Guide to Moths of the British Isles*
Viking, 1984

Wardaugh, A. A.
*Land Snails of the British Isles*
Shire Publications, 2000

Wheater, C. P. & Read, H. J.
*Animals under Logs and Stones*
Richmond Publishing & The Company of Biologists, 1996

Magazines & Journals
All the Wildlife Trusts publish their own magazines and there is the national Wildlife Trusts' magazine, *Natural World*. There are two commercially produced magazines that have features of interest to the garden naturalist. These are *British Wildlife*, Lower Barn, Rooks Farm, Rotherwick, Hook, RG27 9BG (www.britishwildlife.com), and *BBC Wildlife*, Whiteladies Road, Bristol.

# Index